Tea with Jane Austen

Tea with Jane Austen

Recipes inspired by her novels and letters

Pen Vogler

CICO BOOKS

LONDON NEW YORK

www.rylandpeters.com

Published in 2016 by CICO Books
An imprint of Ryland Peters & Small Ltd
20–21 Jockey's Fields   341 E 116th St
London WC1R 4BW   New York, NY 10029

www.rylandpeters.com

20 19 18 17 16 15 14 13 12

A CIP catalog record for this book is available from the
Library of Congress and the British Library.

ISBN: 978-1-78249-342-6

Printed in China

FSC
www.fsc.org
MIX
Paper | Supporting
responsible forestry
FSC® C008047

Copy editor Lee Faber
Designer Sarah Rock
Food photographer Stephen Conroy
Stylist Luis Peral
Home economist Emma Jane Frost
Editor Miriam Catley
In-house designer Fahema Khanam
Art director Sally Powell
Head of production Patricia Harrington
Publishing manager Penny Craig
Publisher Cindy Richards

Notes: All recipes serve four unless indicated otherwise.
All eggs are large (UK medium) unless indicated otherwise.

Contents

INTRODUCTION

If you were invited to "drink tea" with Jane Austen you would be expected, not mid-morning or mid-afternoon, but after the afternoon or early-evening dinner. In Jane's time, fashion remorselessly pushed back the tea hour. From homely Steventon in 1798 she writes to her sister Cassandra, staying at the glamorous Godmersham Park; "We dine now at half-past three, and have done dinner, I suppose, before you begin. We drink tea at half-past six. I am afraid you will despise us."

The "tea-board", together with coffee pots, cakes, and possibly muffins or bread for toasting would be brought into the drawing room by the servants, once the gentlemen had joined the ladies after dinner. This was the time that less honored guests would come and join the party for tea and the rest of the evening's entertainment such as cards and music. Mr Collins almost pops with excitement when her Ladyship invites them, not just "to drink tea and spend the evening at Rosings" but to dine.

Traditionally the hostess or daughters would brew the tea, a ritual that enabled the hostess to display her silver urns, pots, cream jugs, sugar bowls, and delicate china cups and Jane's heroines to conceal their inner turmoil. When the gentlemen finally dine at Longbourn at the end of *Pride and Prejudice*, Miss Bennet makes the tea and Elizabeth, desperate to talk to Darcy and "enraged against herself for being so silly", hardly has patience to pour the coffee. For Fanny Price, the tea-duties at Mansfield Park do no less than deliver her from the "grievous imprisonment of body and mind" of Henry Crawford's attentions.

A close friend, such as Edward Ferrars in *Sense and Sensibility*, might join the Dashwoods for tea at breakfast time; but tea is not part of "morning" calls (which are paid until dinner time). You might, like Miss Bates in *Emma*, press on your guests "sweet-cake from the beaufet" or, while shopping, call into a pastry shop for something delicious (or, to "devour six ices" as does "The Beautifull Cassandra", written by a very youthful Jane). However, a respectable lady would avoid the coffee shops which were still the preserve of men.

Tea, heavily taxed and hugely expensive, was all the rage with those who could afford it. Green tea was pricier and therefore more elegant than black. Some people drank it with cream; a habit which was as odd to Jane as it might be to us. One pleasing trait in an otherwise unappealing acquaintance is that she "drinks no cream in her tea". As with all things fashionable, tea was controversial, with pseudo-scientific essayists denouncing it as "pernicious to health, obstructing industry, and impoverishing the nation". The valetudinarian sisters of *Sanditon* each drink different kinds of herb tea and their brother is horrified to see Charlotte take two cups of strong green tea in one evening; it would render his right side paralysed! Her heroine's arch response about "those who have studied right sides and green tea scientifically", is Jane's amused nod to this topical controversy about tea.

What wasn't controversial is that the cakes, biscuits, muffins, tarts, and 'bunns' that were taken with tea were absolutely delicious. I hope you enjoy trying out the recipes yourself.

BATH BUNS

Mrs. Raffald tells us to "send them in hot for breakfast," which sounds rather indigestible for these rich, buttery buns, and may have been why, when Jane was staying with a rather mean aunt, she joked to Cassandra that she would make herself an inexpensive guest by "disordering my Stomach with Bath bunns." (January 3 1801)

———◆———

Makes 12 cakes

1 lb/450 g all-purpose (plain) flour

1 tsp salt (optional—not in original, but we find yeast buns very bland without it)

⅔ cup/150 g butter

¼ oz/7 g sachet active dried yeast

2 tbsp sugar

1 tbsp caraway seeds

1 cup/225 ml milk

For the glaze

2 tbsp superfine (caster) sugar

1 tbsp milk

Sugar nibs, or a few sugar cubes, roughly crushed and mixed with a few caraway seeds. These are in place of the caraway comfits— sugar-coated caraway seeds—that Mrs. Raffald would have used.

1 Add the salt, if using, to the flour, and rub the butter in until it is like coarse breadcrumbs; sprinkle in the yeast, sugar, and caraway seeds, and mix together well. Warm the milk, and stir it into the dry ingredients to give a soft dough; add a little milk if necessary.

continued >>

2 Give it a good knead for about 10 minutes on a floured surface until it is smooth and pliable; return to the bowl, cover with a cloth, and let it rise in a warm place until double in size; it may take a good 2 or 3 hours because the butter in the dough impedes the rising action of the yeast.

3 Punch the air out of the dough and make up 12 cakes. Put them onto greased baking sheets, cover with a damp dish towel (tea towel) or plastic wrap (clingfilm) and leave to rise again for up to 1 hour.

4 Preheat the oven to 375°F/190°C/Gas Mark 5.

5 Bake for 12–15 minutes until they are golden brown.

6 Heat together the milk and sugar for the glaze, and brush it over the hot buns, then strew the crushed sugar cubes and caraway seeds over the top.

Bath Cakes

Rub half a pound of butter into a pound of flour, and one spoonful of good barm. Warm some cream and make it into a light paste, set it to the fire to rise. When you make them up take four ounces of caraway comfits, work part of them in and strew the rest on the top. Make them into round cakes the size of a French roll. Bake them on sheet tins and send them in hot for breakfast.

ELIZABETH RAFFALD
The Experienced English Housekeeper, 1769

ENGLISH MUFFINS

Mr. Woodhouse comments on Emma passing the muffins to her guests an overattentive (and indigestible) twice. Muffins were also served with after-dinner tea in *Pride and Prejudice* and in *The Watsons*. Traditionally they were toasted front and back (not in the middle) and pulled (not cut) apart around the waist and, of course, laden with butter.

———◆———

Makes 12 muffins

1 lb/450 g strong bread flour

¼ oz/7 g sachet active dried yeast

1 tsp salt (optional—not in original, but we find yeast buns very bland without it)

2 tbsp/25 g butter

Generous 1¼ cups/280 ml milk

1 egg

1 Mix the yeast and salt, if using, into the flour and make a well in the center. Warm the butter in the milk until it melts. Beat the egg and pour into the center of the flour; add the milk, and draw the flour in from the edges until you have a dough.

2 Knead it on a floured surface until it is smooth, then return the dough to the bowl, cover it with a clean dish (tea) towel and leave to rise in a warm place until double in size—about 45–60 minutes. Punch out the air and make the dough into a flat cake about ⅜-inch/1 cm high on a floured board, and cut out circular cakes with a cookie (biscuit) cutter. Let them rise again in a warm place on a lightly floured baking sheet for half an hour. Heat a griddle or heavy-based frying pan with very little oil or lard, and griddle them for 8–10 minutes each side on low to medium heat.

Muffins

Mix two pounds of flour with two eggs,
two ounces of butter melted in a pint of milk,
and four or five spoonfuls of yeast: beat it
thoroughly, and set it to rise two or three hours.
Bake on a hot hearth, in flat cakes. When done
on one side turn them. Note: Muffins, rolls,
or bread, if stale, may be made to taste new,
by dipping in cold water, and toasting, or
heating in an oven, or Dutch oven, till
the outside be crisp.

MRS. RUNDELL
A New System of Domestic Cookery, 1806

SALLY LUNNS

Sally Lunns were warm and golden bread cakes, eaten at breakfast with butter or clotted cream—even more extravagant than the rich French bread that General Tilney served in *Northanger Abbey*. Legend has it that they were named after their inventor, Solange Luyon, a French Huguenot refugee who worked at a bakery in Bath.

———◦◉◦———

Makes 6 cakes

¼ oz/7 g sachet active dried yeast

2 tbsp superfine (caster) sugar

2 eggs plus optional extra egg white for glazing

Generous 1¼ cups/280 ml cream or milk

1 lb/450 g strong bread flour

1 tsp salt (optional—not in original, but we find yeast buns very bland without it)

Butter or clotted cream, to serve

1 Blend the yeast with the sugar and beat it thoroughly with the eggs and cream. Sift in the flour and salt, if using, to make a dough that is smooth, but not sticky (add a little milk if it feels too dry.)

2 Knead it on a floured surface for about 10 minutes until it feels elastic. Put it back in the bowl, cover with a clean dish towel (tea towel) and let it rise for 1½ hours.

3 Punch the air out of the dough and divide it into 6 cakes (you may find it helpful to flour your hands.) Lay the cakes on a greased baking sheet.

4 Cover and let them rise again until double in size—30 minutes to 1 hour.

5 Preheat the oven to 400°F/200°C/Gas Mark 6. Glaze them with egg white or milk if you fancy it, and bake for 12–15 minutes.

6 Serve with butter or clotted cream.

Note: Margaret Dods warms a little saffron in the milk or cream to improve the color, but organic eggs with good orangey yellow yolks should make them properly golden.

Sally Lunn Cakes

Make them as French bread, but dissolve some sugar in the hot milk. Mould into the form of cakes. A little saffron boiled in the milk enriches the colour of these or any other cakes.

MARGARET DODS
The Cook and Housewife's Manual, 1826

BUTTER BUNS

For a cosy fireside tea, people would toast and lavish
butter on these "butter buns", which we know as teacakes.
Martha's recipe is quite plain, but the cookery writer Mrs.
Rundell suggests flavoring them with nutmeg, Jamaica
peppers (allspice), caraway, or rosewater.

———◆———

Makes 12 teacakes

1 lb/450 g strong white bread flour

¼ cup/50 g sugar

¼ oz/7 g sachet active dried yeast

1 tsp salt (optional—not in original but we find yeast
buns very bland without it)

½ stick/50 g butter, diced

Handful of currants

1¼ cups/285 ml milk

2 egg yolks

Optional flavorings

1 tsp nutmeg and/or 1 tsp allspice

1 tbsp caraway seeds

2 tsp of natural rosewater (with no added alcohol)

1 Put the flour, sugar, yeast, and salt, if using, into a large bowl
and mix well. If you are flavoring with the nutmeg and/or
allspice, or the caraway seeds, mix them in at the same time.

2 Rub in the butter until the mixture resembles breadcrumbs,
then stir in the currants. Warm the milk to blood heat and lightly
beat in the 2 egg yolks, and the rosewater for flavoring, if using.

3 Make a well in the flour, pour in the milk mixture, and draw the flour into the liquid to make a soft dough. Knead on a floured board for 10 minutes; if it is too sticky, add a little flour, but keep it as supple and moist as possible.

4 Return it to the bowl; cover with a dish (tea) towel and let it rise in a warm place for an hour.

5 Punch out the air, and on a floured board, make into 12 buns and flatten each slightly; then put them on a large baking sheet greased with butter. Cover them again with a dish (tea) towel, lightly dampened, and let them rise again until double in size—about 45 minutes in a warm place or overnight in the fridge.

6 Preheat the oven to 400°F/200°C/Gas Mark 6 and bake the buns for 15 minutes until golden brown on top.

Butter Buns

Put ¼ lb of butter into 2 lbs of flour, a ¼ lb of sugar, a handful of currants, two spoonfuls of good yeast. Set it to rise before the fire. Add the yokes of two eggs and about a pint of warm milk, mix into a limp paste and make it into forty buns.

MARTHA LLOYD'S HOUSEHOLD BOOK

ROUT CAKES

Mrs. Elton, in *Emma*, professes herself a little shocked at her unsophisticated new neighbors, particularly the lack of ice at card parties, the want of two drawing rooms, and "the poor attempt at rout-cakes." These are a little like elegant rock buns, with the typical eighteenth-century taste of flowers and spirits.

——◆——

Makes 12 little cakes

¾ cup/100 g self-rising flour

½ stick/50 g butter

¼ cup/50 g sugar

⅓ cup/50 g currants

1 egg

1 tsp natural orange flower water (with no added alcohol)

1 tsp natural rosewater (with no added alcohol)

1 tbsp brandy

1 Preheat the oven to 375°F/190°C/Gas Mark 5.

2 Rub the butter into the flour and add the sugar and currants. Whisk the egg with the orange flower water, rosewater, and brandy.

3 Add the egg mixture to the flour a little at a time, mixing until you have a paste that is sticky, but holds its shape; you may not need all the liquid.

4 Put heaping teaspoonsful of the mixture onto greased baking sheets and bake for 10–12 minutes.

Rout Drop Cakes

Mix two pounds of flour, one ditto butter, one ditto sugar, one ditto currants, clean and dry; then wet into a stiff paste with two eggs, a large spoonful of orange-flower water, ditto rose-water, ditto sweet wine, ditto brandy; drop on a tin-plate floured, a very short time bakes them.

MRS. RUNDELL
A New System of Domestic Cookery, 1806

PLUM CAKE

"Plum" means dried fruit, and rich plum cakes were made for Twelfth Night revels and weddings. Mr. Woodhouse tries to persuade Mr. Perry, the apothecary, that they are indigestible. "There was a strange rumour in Highbury of all the little Perrys being seen with a slice of Mrs. Weston's wedding-cake in their hands: but Mr. Woodhouse would never believe it."

———◦●◦———

1¼ cups/170 g currants

1¼ cups/170 g raisins

2 tbsp/30 ml brandy

2 tbsp/30 ml sweet wine

1¾ cups/225 g self-rising flour

¾ tsp ground mace

¾ tsp grated nutmeg

½ tsp ground cloves

½ tsp ground allspice

2 sticks/225 g butter

1 heaping cup/225 g soft dark brown sugar

Grated zest of ½ lemon

4 eggs, beaten

Heaping ½ cup/60 g ground almonds

¾ cup/60 g slivered (flaked) almonds

¼ cup/60 ml cream or milk

1 Leave the dried fruit to soak in the brandy and wine overnight.

2 Preheat the oven to 300°F/150°C/Gas Mark 2.

3 Sift the flour and spices together.

4 Cream the butter with the sugar and lemon zest until pale and fluffy. Beat in the eggs, a little at a time; if the mixture starts to curdle, throw in a little flour to stabilize it.

5 Fold in the remaining flour and then stir in the rest of the ingredients.

6 Butter a deep 8-inch/20 cm cake pan with a removable base, and line it with 2 thicknesses of parchment paper. Line the outside with two thicknesses of foil or brown paper, tied with string.

7 Spoon the mixture into the pan and bake for 3 hours, or until a toothpick inserted into the center comes out clean. If it starts to brown too early, cover with layers of foil or parchment paper.

Plum Cakes

Mix thoroughly a quarter of a peck of fine
flour, well dried, with a pound of dry and
sifted loaf sugar, three pounds of currants
washed and very dry, half a pound of raisins
stoned and chopped, a quarter of an ounce of
mace and cloves, twenty Jamaica peppers, a
grated nutmeg, the peel of a lemon cut as fine
as possible, and half a pound of almonds
blanched and beaten with orange-flower water.
Melt two pounds of butter in a pint and a
quarter of cream, but not hot; put to it a pint
of sweet wine, a glass of brandy, the whites and
yolks of twelve eggs beaten apart, and half a
pint of good yeast. Strain this liquid by degrees
into the dry ingredients, beating them together
a full hour, then butter the hoop, or pan, and
bake it. As you put the batter into the hoop,
or pan, throw in plenty of citron, lemon,
and orange-candy.

If you ice the cake, take half a pound of double-refined sugar sifted, and put a little with the white of an egg, beat it well, and by degrees pour in the remainder. It must be whisked near an hour, with the addition of a little orange-flower water, but mind not to put much. When the cake is done, pour the iceing over, and return it to the oven for fifteen minutes; but if the oven be warm, keep it near the mouth, and the door open, lest the colour be spoiled.

MRS. RUNDELL
A New System of Domestic Cookery, 1806

RATAFIA CAKES

Martha Lloyd suggests making these macaroon-like
biscuits with apricot kernels or bitter almonds. Both
have an excellent flavor but, less desirably, contain small
amounts of cyanide (bitter almonds are banned, but
apricot kernels are still available.) To get that distinctive
nutty taste, use natural almond extract, which is made
from bitter almonds with the cyanide removed.

———◦◉◦———

Makes 25–30 small cookies

2¼ cups/225 g ground almonds

1⅔ cups/225 g confectioners' (icing) sugar

3 egg whites

2–3 drops natural almond extract or 1 tbsp
Amaretto plus 1 extra tbsp ground almonds

1 Preheat the oven to 325°F/160°C/Gas Mark 3.

2 Put the ground almonds in a bowl, sift in the confectioners'
sugar and mix well.

3 Whisk the egg whites until they form soft peaks, beating in the
almond extract or Amaretto at the end; and then fold them into
the almond mixture until you have a smooth paste. If you've
used Amaretto, you may need to add a few more almonds to get
the texture right.

4 Put heaping teaspoonsful onto baking parchment on baking
sheets, and bake for 12–15 minutes until golden brown.

Ratafia Cakes

Take 8oz of apricot kernels, if they
cannot be had bitter almonds will do as well.
Blanch them and beat them very fine with
a little orange flower water, mix them with the
whites of three eggs well beaten and put to them 2lbs
of single refined sugar finely beaten and sifted.
Work all together and it will be like a paste, then
lay it in little round bits on tin plates flour'd.
Set them in an oven which is not very hot and
they will puff up and soon be baked.

MARTHA LLOYD'S HOUSEHOLD BOOK

JUMBLES

Fanny, from *Mansfield Park*, enjoyed biscuits (cookies) after (or instead of) dinner and, in *Emma*, Mr. Woodhouse offered them to Mrs. Bates with tea (along with baked apples and wine.) These jumbles are old-fashioned cookies that were originally made from stiff dough and tied in knot shapes. By Georgian times they were simply dropped from a spoon and baked on cookie sheets.

———●———

Makes approx. 20 cookies (biscuits)

1⅓ cups/175 g all-purpose (plain) flour

½ tsp baking powder

1 stick/125 g butter

1 cup/150 g light brown sugar

Zest of 1 lemon

1 egg, well beaten

1 Preheat the oven to 350°F/180°C/Gas Mark 4.

2 Sift the flour and baking powder into a bowl.

3 Gently melt the butter over low heat, add the sugar and lemon zest.

4 Whisk the egg into the butter mixture, then pour into the center of the flour, mixing well to combine the ingredients.

5 Drop the mixture in heaping teaspoonsful onto well-buttered or silicone baking sheets, giving them plenty of room to spread out.

6 Bake for 10–12 minutes.

Jumbles

Rasp on some good sugar the rinds of
two lemons; dry, reduce it to powder, and sift
it with as much more as will make up a pound
in weight: mix with it one pound of flour, four
well-beaten eggs, and six ounces of warm butter:
drop the mixture on buttered tins, and bake the
jumbles in a very slow oven from twenty to
thirty minutes. They should be pale,
but perfectly crisp.

ELIZA ACTON
Modern Cookery for Private Families, 1845

JANE'S SPONGE CAKE

The *Oxford English Dictionary* notes that the first recorded use of the word "sponge-cake" is by Jane, writing to Cassandra (June 15 1808): "You know how interesting the purchase of a sponge-cake is to me." Its other name, "pound cake," referred to the quantity of each ingredient, an easy way to remember the recipe when many cooks couldn't read. Mercifully, Martha's recipe has just half a pound of sugar.

2 sticks/225 g butter

Heaping ½ cup/110 g superfine (caster) sugar

4 eggs

1¾ cups/225 g all-purpose (plain) flour

1 tsp baking powder (optional—not in original but it gives a lighter result)

Pinch of salt (optional—not in original but it helps bring out the flavors)

¼ cup/25 g caraway seeds

Eliza Acton notes that a sponge cake may be flavored "with lemon rind, or with bitter almonds, vanilla, or confected orange-blossoms reduced to powder," so you could omit the caraway and use one of the flavorings below:

Zest of 1 lemon

½ tsp natural almond extract

½ tsp natural vanilla extract or use vanilla sugar instead of the superfine sugar

Zest of 1 orange, plus 1 tsp natural orange flower water (with no added alcohol)

1 Preheat the oven to 325°F/160°C/Gas Mark 3.

2 Cream the butter and sugar until pale and fluffy. Whisk the eggs well and add them a little at a time to the butter. If the mixture starts to curdle, add a spoonful of flour.

3 Sift the flour, baking powder, and salt together, and fold into the butter and egg mixture with the caraway seeds or other flavoring.

4 Grease and line an 8-inch/20 cm round cake pan and spoon the mixture in. Tap the pan sharply on the work surface a couple of time to release the bubbles.

5 Bake for 50–60 minutes until a toothpick (skewer) inserted in the center comes out clean.

A Pound Cake

Take a lb of fine flour well dried. Then take a lb of butter and work it very well with your hands till it is soft. Then work into it half a pound of sugar. Then take 12 eggs putting away half the whites, then work them also into your butter and sugar. Then strew your flour into your butter, sugar and eggs, by little and little, till all be in, then strew in 2 oz of caraway seeds. Butter your pan and bake it in a quick oven, - an hour and a half will bake it.

MARTHA LLOYD'S HOUSEHOLD BOOK

GINGERBREAD

Emma Woodhouse, waiting for Harriet Smith in Highbury, notices the homey details of the High Street, including "a string of dawdling children round the baker's little bow-window eyeing the gingerbread." In Martha's recipe, the caraway seeds work really well, but we would find using just molasses (black treacle,) as she does, quite intense.

Makes 24–30 cookies (biscuits)

2½ cups/340 g all-purpose (plain) flour

1 tsp baking soda (bicarbonate of soda)

2 heaping tsp ground ginger (or 3 if you like a bit more fire)

½ tsp ground nutmeg

¼ tsp ground cloves (optional—not in Martha's recipe but an excellent ingredient in old gingerbread recipes)

½ cup/100 g soft brown sugar

1 tbsp caraway seeds

4 tbsp light corn (golden) syrup

1 tbsp molasses (black treacle)

1 stick/125 g butter

2 tsp brandy

1 egg, beaten

Candied orange peel (optional)

1 Preheat the oven to 350°F/180°C/Gas Mark 4.

2 Sift the flour, baking soda, and spices into a bowl and stir in the sugar and caraway seeds.

continued >>

3 Put the syrups into a saucepan, using a heated spoon. Warm gently, add the butter, and when it is just melted, add the brandy, and then the beaten egg.

4 Make a well in the flour and gradually pour the treacle mixture in, gathering the flour from the edges of the bowl.

5 Leave it to cool in the fridge for 20–30 minutes. You should end up with a stiff dough; if it is cracking, add a little more brandy or water, or a little more flour if it is too sticky.

6 Roll it out to ⅛–¼-inch/4–5 mm depth on a well-floured board and cut out round "cakes" with a cookie cutter. When you have put these on a greased baking sheet, as Martha says, "You may add what sweetmeats you please." Pieces of candied orange peel work especially well with the spices and caraway.

7 Bake for 8–10 minutes, but watch them like a hawk as they burn very easily.

Gingerbread

Take four pints of flour rub into it 3 quarters of a pd of butter 2 oz of Ginger a Nutmeg. one oz of Carraway seeds a quarter of a pint of Brandy. 2 pd of treacle. mix it altogether; & let it lay till it grows stiff then roll it out. & cut it into cakes. you may add what sweetmeats you please.

MARTHA LLOYD'S HOUSEHOLD BOOK

LEMON CHEESECAKES

Jane wrote to Cassandra about "a good dinner" she had at Devizes while traveling: "amongst other things we had asparagus and a lobster, which made me wish for you, and some cheesecakes..." (Letter, May 17 1799.) Georgian recipes for cheesecakes often contained no cheese; these are little egg custards enriched with almonds.

———

Makes about 12 cakes

1 batch of shortcrust pastry or sweet rich shortcrust pastry (see recipes on pages 60–61)

½ stick/50 g butter

½ cup/100 g superfine (caster) sugar

Zest of 1 large or 2 small lemons

2 whole eggs, plus 1 yolk

2 tsp natural orange flower water (without alcohol)

1 tbsp cream

1 cup/100 g ground almonds

1 Preheat the oven to 375°F/190°C/Gas Mark 5.

2 Roll out the pastry, and cut it into circles to line tartlet pans of about ¾-inch/2 cm depth.

3 Cream the butter and sugar with most of the lemon zest until pale and fluffy.

4 Whisk the eggs with the orange flower water and cream until frothy, then add them bit by bit to the butter and sugar mixture; if it starts to separate, add a few ground almonds. Stir in the ground almonds at the end.

continued >>

5 Spoon the mixture into the pastry cases, leaving a little space at the top for it to rise slightly. Bake for 10–15 minutes until golden and firm on top.

6 Decorate the cakes with the remaining lemon zest.

Lemon Cheesecakes

Take ½ lb of almonds, blanch'd in cold water, let stand all night, beat fine with orange flower water. Take ½ lb of fine sugar. Then take the peel of two lemons, paired very thin, boil it in water till they are very tender and not bitter; then beat it very fine in a mortar with the sugar, then mix it with the almonds. Take eight eggs (leaving out half the whites); take ¼ lb of butter, melted, and let it be cold, then mix altogether. Bake it in a fine paste in small patty pans, put some sugar to your paste.

MARTHA LLOYD'S HOUSEHOLD BOOK

STRAWBERRY TARTLETS

In one of the funniest passages in *Emma*, Mrs. Elton, picking strawberries at Donwell Abbey, gushes about "the best fruit in England", but downgrades them to "too rich... inferior to cherries" as she wearies in the sun. These summery tarts are filled with a strawberry fool; a lovely way to use up any squishy fruit. This combines Eliza Acton's recipes for "strawberry tartlets" which are too delicate to carry out on a picnic, with her more robust crème pâtissière, or pastry cream.

Makes 4 small tarts or 1 large tart

1 batch of shortcrust pastry or sweet rich shortcrust pastry (see recipes on pages 60–61)

1 egg, beaten

1 pint/200 g soft or damaged strawberries, hulled

3 egg yolks

¼ cup/50 g superfine (caster) sugar

Heaping ¼ cup/40 g all-purpose (plain) flour

1¼ cups/300 ml milk

Extra berries to decorate

1 You will need 4 x 4-inch/10-cm tartlet pans or one 9-inch/22-cm pie pan.

2 Preheat the oven to 400°F/200°C/Gas Mark 6.

3 Roll out your shortcrust pastry to about ¼-inch/5 mm thickness and use it to line four well-greased pans (or single pan, if using), leaving about ¼-inch/5 mm pastry above the edge

continued >>

of the pans to allow for shrinkage. Paint the bottom of each with beaten egg, prick with a fork, and bake blind for 10–12 minutes for the tartlets or 15–18 minutes for the large tart. Reduce the temperature to 375°F/190°C/Gas Mark 5.

4 Crush the strawberries in a dish, and set aside as the juice runs out.

5 Beat the egg yolks and sugar in a heavy bowl until the mixture is pale yellow, and the sugar has dissolved. Sift in the flour, a third at a time, beating vigorously after each addition. Boil the milk, then pour it gradually onto the flour mixture, beating it in as you go. Return the custard to the pan, and reheat it gently to boiling point, beating thoroughly, until it holds its shape. Take off the heat, stir in the crushed strawberries and pour into the pastry cases. Bake for 10–15 minutes.

6 When cool, decorate with half strawberries.

38

Strawberry Tartlets

Take a half pint of freshly-gathered
strawberries, without the stalks: first crush,
and then mix them with two ounces and a half
of powdered sugar, stir to them by degrees four
well-whisked eggs, beat the mixture a little, and
put it into patty-pans lined with fine paste:
they should only be three parts filled. Bake the
tartlets from ten to twelve minutes.

ELIZA ACTON
Modern Cookery for Private Families, 1845

GOOSEBERRY TART

Poor ten-year-old Fanny Price, arriving at
Mansfield Park for the first time, is so exhausted and
homesick that "vain was even the sight of a gooseberry
tart towards giving her comfort." Recipes of the time were
either for summer pies made with fresh gooseberries
or all-year-round tarts made with jam.

———◆———

Makes 4 small tarts or 1 large tart

1 lb/450 g gooseberries

1–1½ cups/200–300 g superfine (caster) sugar
per 2 lb/1 kg of gooseberries

Double batch of shortcrust pastry (see recipe on page 60)

1 Wash, then top and tail the gooseberries.

2 Put the gooseberries in a saucepan with a tablespoon of water
and simmer very gently until the skins start to break—about
5–8 minutes. Then add sugar, starting with ½ cup/100 g per
1 lb/450 g of fruit and adding a little more if it needs it, and
simmer for a couple of minutes more.

3 Preheat the oven to 375°F/190°C/Gas Mark 5.

4 Roll the pastry out and cut into two pieces, one twice as large
as the other. Use the larger piece to line a 9–10-inch/22–25 cm
round metal pie pan with pastry. Roll the smaller piece out and
cut into strips of about ¾-inch/2 cm wide. Pour in the fruit and
make a lattice pattern on the top with the pastry strips.

5 Bake for 30 minutes until the pastry is golden.

Gooseberry Jam for Tarts

Gather your gooseberries (the clear white or green sort) when ripe; top and tail, and weigh them; a pound to three quarters of a pound of fine sugar, add half a pint of water; boil and skim the sugar and water; then put the fruit, and boil gently till clear; then break and put into small pots.

MRS. RUNDELL
A New System of Domestic Cookery, 1806

BUTTERED APPLE TART

Mr. Woodhouse reassures Miss Bates that he is offering
her a tart made from fresh apples and "You need not be
afraid of unwholesome preserves here. I do not advise the
custard." I hope you disregard Mr. Woodhouse's views on
custard and enjoy Hannah Glasse's unusual but happy
marriage of egg custard and apple tart.

———◆———

4–5 cooking apples

2 tbsp/30 g butter

2–4 tbsp sugar

½ tsp grated nutmeg

½ tsp ground cinnamon (optional—not in original recipe)

Juice and zest of 1 orange

1 batch of Sweet Rich Shortcrust Pastry (see recipe page 61)

3 eggs, separated

Confectioners' (icing) sugar, to serve

1 Skin, core, and slice the apples and cook them in a
tablespoon of water until just soft. While the apples are hot,
stir in the butter, sugar to taste, the nutmeg, and cinnamon if
using, and the orange zest and juice.

2 While the mixture cools, preheat the oven to 375°F/190°C/
Gas Mark 5, and line a 10-inch/25 cm pie dish with the pastry.

3 Beat the egg yolks and stir them into the apple. Whisk the
egg whites to stiff peaks and fold them into the mixture. Pour
the mixture into the pastry case and bake for approximately
30 minutes until the eggs are set.

4 Serve with a dusting of confectioners' sugar over it.

A Buttered Tort

Take eight or ten large Codlings and scald
them, when cold skin them, take the Pulp and
beat it as fine as you can with a Silver
Spoon, then mix in the Yolks of six Eggs, and
the Whites of four beat all well together, a
Seville Orange squeez'd in the Juice, and
shread the rind as fine as possible, some
grated Nutmeg and Sugar to your Taste; melt
some fresh butter, and beat up with it
according as it wants, till it is all like a
fine thick Cream, then make a fine Puff-paste,
have a large Tin Patty, that will just hold
it, cover the Patty with the Paste, and pour
in the Ingredients, don't put any Cover on,
bake it a quarter of an Hour, then flip it out
of the Patty on to a Dish, and throw fine
Sugar well beat all over it. It is a very
pretty Side-dish for a second Course. You may
make this of any large Apple you please.

HANNAH GLASSE
The Art of Cookery Made Plain and Easy, 1747

MINCE PIES

Mince pies were originally made with mutton, beef, or tongue, but this was becoming optional by the eighteenth century. "If you chuse Meat in your Pies, parboil a Neat's-Tongue, peel it, and chop the Meat as fine as possible, and mix with the rest," writes Hannah. Hers is quite a boozy mincemeat; delicious! She suggests making several small pies or, as we do here, one slightly larger one.

———◆———

Makes one big pie

For the mincemeat

Scant ½ cup/100 g suet, shredded

7 oz/200 g apples, cored and chopped

1 heaping cup/150 g raisins

Heaping 1½ cups/160 g currants

¼ cup/50 g brown sugar

1 tsp ground mace

¼ tsp ground cloves

½ tsp nutmeg

3 tbsp/45 ml brandy

3 tbsp/45 ml sherry

For the pie

Double batch of shortcrust pastry (see recipe on page 60)

A neat's tongue (a beef [ox] tongue) or about 1¼ cups/200 g boiled beef or tongue, chopped small (optional)

Scant ½ cup/50 g candied peel

Zest of 1 orange

Juice of ½ lemon or ½ orange

2 tbsp/30 ml red wine

continued >>

1 Make the mincemeat by mixing together the suet, apples, dried fruit, sugar, spices, brandy, and sherry.

2 Preheat the oven to 400°F/200°C/Gas Mark 6.

3 Line a pie dish with shortcrust pastry, then add the following: a thin layer of meat (such as beef or tongue, chopped small); a thin layer of citron (candied peel will do); a good layer of mincemeat; a layer of thinly cut orange zest; finishing with a thin layer of meat.

4 Mix together the juice of half a lemon or half an orange with 2 tablespoons of red wine and sprinkle this over, before covering with a pastry lid.

5 Bake for 25–35 minutes.

Variation: Lemon mincemeat, a pleasant, light version, was popular for Christmas pies. It was made with the addition of a lemon boiled and mashed to a pulp. Martha Lloyd has a recipe for it, and so does Duncan MacDonald, the cook at the Bedford Tavern in London's Covent Garden and author of *The New London Family Cook*. Jane knew of the tavern; in *Northanger Abbey*, John Thorpe tries to impress Catherine by saying he knows General Tilney because "I have met him forever at the Bedford."

To make Mince-Pies the best Way

Take three Pounds of Suet shread very fine, and chopped as small as possible, two Pounds of raisings stoned, and chopped as fine as possible, two Pounds of Currans, nicely picked, washed,

rubbed, and dried at the Fire, half a hundred
of fine Pippins, pared, cored, and chopped small,
half a Pound of fine Sugar pounded fine, a
quarter of an Ounce of Mace, a quarter of an
Ounce of Cloves, two large Nutmegs, all beat
fine; put all together into a great Pan, and
mix it well together with half a Pint of
Brandy, and half a Pint of Sach: put it down
close in a Stone-pot, and it will keep good four
Months. When you make your Pies, take a little
Dish, something bigger than a Soop-plate, lay a
very thin Crust all over it, lay a thin Layer of
Meat, And then a thin layer of Citron cut very
thin, then a Layer of Mince meat, and a thin
Layer of Orange-peel cut thin, over that a
little Meat; squeeze half the Juice of a fine
Seville Orange, or Lemon, and pour in three
Spoonfuls of Red Wine; lay on your Crust, and
bake it nicely.

HANNAH GLASSE
The Art of Cookery Made Plain and Easy, 1747

CHERRIES EN CHEMISE

In *Sense and Sensibility*, when Willoughby rejects Marianne in favor of the wealthy Miss Grey, well-meaning Mrs. Jennings seeks to cure her broken heart with olives and dried cherries. This recipe from Margaret Dods part-dries the cherries and makes an uplifting gift for a friend, whether broken hearted or not.

———◈———

1⅔ cups/250 g fresh ripe cherries with stems

1–2 egg whites

Confectioners' (icing) sugar or superfine (caster) sugar

For the meringue

2 egg whites

¼ cup/50 g superfine (caster) sugar

1 Take large, ripe cherries and cut off the stems with scissors, leaving about 1-inch/2 cm to each cherry.

2 Beat an egg white until it is frothy, and roll the cherries in the egg and then in confectioners' (icing) sugar.

3 Place them on parchment paper, and let them dry at room temperature until the "frosting" adheres. They should keep for about a week.

4 They are too delicate to transport, though, so for a gift that will go in a box, make meringues to surround them. Beat the egg whites until they are stiff, and fold in the superfine (caster) sugar. Pile teaspoonsful of the mixture onto parchment paper, and place half a pitted cherry on top. Leave some uncovered, and cover some with another blob of meringue. Turn the oven to 225°F/110°C/Gas Mark ¼. Give them 2½–3 hours to dry out in the oven.

Cherries En Chemise.

Take the largest ripe cherries you can
get. Cut off the stalks with scissors,
leaving about an inch to each cherry. Beat
the white of an egg to a froth, and roll
them in it one by one, and then roll them
lightly in sifted sugar. Lay a sheet of
paper on a sieve reversed, and laying them
on this, set them on a stove till they are
to be served. Obs the same may be done
with bunches of currants, strawberries,
hautboys, etc. Fruits en chemise look
well and cost little.

MARGARET DODS
The Cook and Housewife's Manual, 1826

APRICOT MARMALADE
AND APRICOT "CAKES"

In *Sense and Sensibility*, Lady Middleton successfully
deploys "apricot marmalade" (which we would now call
jam) to stop her daughter's attention-seeking screams. The
apricot cakes are made from a thick purée, which is dried
in the oven to make delicious, chewy sweets.

———◆◆◆———

Makes 2 quarts/2 litres

18 oz/500 g fresh apricots or dried apricots,
reconstituted overnight in apple juice (drained weight)

1¼ cups/250 g preserving sugar for marmalade/1¾ cups/350 g
preserving sugar for cakes

1 Pit the fruit and boil it until tender—about 30 minutes.
Then rub through a sieve or purée in a blender, stir in the sugar
and bring back to a boil. Boil until the sugar has dissolved.

2 To make apricot cakes, spoon the mixture into oiled muffin
cups and smooth down. Leave in a very low oven,
175°F/80°C/Gas Mark ¼ (or lower if possible) to dry out for
5–6 hours, turning them over halfway. If using Gas Mark ¼,
check the cakes after a couple of hours.

Apricot Marmalade

When you preserve your apricots, pick out all the bad ones and those that are too ripe for keeping. Boil them in the syrup until they will mash, then beat them in a mortar to a paste. Take half their weight of loaf sugar and put as much water to it as will dissolve it, boil it and skim it well. Boil them till they look clear and the syrup thick like a fine jelly, then put it into your sweetmeat glasses and keep them for use.

Apricot Paste Pare and stone your apricots, boil them in water till they will mash quite small. Put a pound of double-refined sugar in your preserving pan with as much water as will dissolve it, and boil it to sugar again. Take it off the stove and put in a pound of apricots, let it stand till the sugar is melted. Then make it scalding hot, but don't let it boil. Pour it into china dishes or cups, set them in a stove. When they are stiff enough to turn out put them on glass plates. Turn them as you see occasion till they are dry.

ELIZABETH RAFFALD
The Experienced English Housekeeper, 1769

A HEDGEHOG

This delicate marzipan is made into a hedgehog with
almonds for the spines and dried currants for eyes.
Although we might make it for a child's birthday, it would
have been made to amuse adult guests, served on a pool
of flavored cream or jelly.

———◦◦◦———

2½ cups/250 g ground almonds

¾–1 cup/120–140 g confectioner's (icing) sugar

A little natural orange flower or rosewater (with no added alcohol)
or orange juice

Half almonds or slivered (flaked) almonds

Currants for the eyes (and nose, if you like)

1 Preheat the oven to 350°F/180°C/Gas Mark 4.

2 Mix the ground almonds and sugar well together; add the
liquid, a teaspoonful at a time, until you have a thick, moldable
paste that doesn't crack (like marzipan).

3 Hannah makes this paste into one big hedgehog, using almonds
for the spines, and currants for the eyes. I think it is nicer to make
it into little ones (or one bigger one and a few little ones) and
bake them for 10 minutes or so until the outsides are golden
brown. This is the sweetmeat called "marchpane" in Tudor times;
it has a lovely, chewy texture and is nicer than raw marzipan.

4 To serve: Hannah suggests surrounding it with a fine
Hartshorn Jelly (not recommended) or a mixture of cream, wine,
and orange juice. To make a green jelly in the traditional way,
color the jelly with a little spinach juice. Don't worry—you can't
taste the spinach through the lemon and sugar in the recipe!

A Hedgehog

Take two Quarts of sweet blanched Almonds, beat
them well in a Mortar, with a little Canary and
Orange-flower Water, to keep them from oiling.
Make them into a stiff Paste, then beat in, Sugar,
put in half a Pound of sweet Butter melted, set
on a Furnace, or slow Fire, and keep it constantly
stirring till it is stiff enough to be made into the
Form of a Hedge-Hog, then put it into a Dish.

HANNAH GLASSE
The Art of Cookery Made Plain and Easy, 1747

TOASTED CHEESE

When Fanny Price leaves Mansfield Park to stay with her parents, she finds their house a maelstrom of people; her father calling for rum and water, her little brothers begging for toasted cheese for supper. Jane remarks to Cassandra on the hospitality of a gentleman who "made a point of ordering toasted cheese for supper entirely on my account." (Letter, August 27 1805.)

Makes four pieces

4 whole salted anchovies or 8–12 anchovy fillets

4 slices sourdough or Italian bread, such as ciabatta

A little olive oil

Garlic clove (optional)

7 oz/200 g Parmesan cheese or other strong cheese, such as mature Cheddar, grated

1 Put a baking tray in the oven and preheat to 400°F/200°C/Gas Mark 6.

2 Rinse the anchovies and pat them dry with paper towel. Drizzle a little olive oil on the breads and, if you like, rub them with the cut side of a garlic clove.

3 Cut the whole anchovies longways into two and lay them or the fillets on the bread. Put them on the hot baking tray, cover with the grated cheese, and bake for about 10–12 minutes until the cheese is melted and the edges are browned.

4 Alternatively, toast one side of the bread, lay the anchovies and cheese (with oil and optional garlic) on the untoasted side as before, and let it brown under the broiler (grill) for 5–6 minutes.

Anchovies with Parmesan Cheese

Fry some bits of bread about the length of an anchovy in good oil or butter, lay the half of an anchovy, with the bone upon each bit, and strew over them some Parmesan cheese grated fine, and colour them nicely in an oven, or with a salamander*, squeeze the juice of an orange or lemon, and pile them up in your dish and send them to table. This seems to be but a trifling thing, but I never saw it come whole from table.

WILLIAM VERRAL
A Complete System of Cookery, 1759

* A salamander was an iron disc with a wooden handle, heated in the coals until it glowed red, and then held over dishes to broil (grill) them.

57

CHOCOLATE TO DRINK

Chocolate wasn't yet eaten as a solid sweet, but, like cocoa, taken as a drink, luxurious enough to be served at a wedding breakfast Jane attended. It was grated from a solid block and gadget-lovers such as the General would have had a special chocolate mill to give it a fine froth—quite a palaver as the original recipe shows!

Makes One Pot

3½ oz/100 g bittersweet (plain) good-quality
chocolate (70% cocoa solids)

1¾ cups/400 ml milk or milk and light (single) cream

1 Chop the chocolate into very small pieces or, even better, grate it into a mixing bowl.

2 Warm the milk or milk and cream to just below boiling point, then turn off the heat.

3 Whisk in the chocolate.

4 Serve in coffee cups or small teacups.

Chocolate

Those who use much of this article, will
find the following mode of preparing it
both useful and economical:

Cut a cake of chocolate in very small bits;
put a pint of water into the pot, and when
it boils, put in the above; mill it off the
fire until quite melted, then on a gentle
fire till it boils; pour it in a basin, and
it will keep in a cool place eight or ten
days or more. When wanted, put a spoonful
or two into milk, boil it with sugar, and
mill it well. This, if not made thick,
is a very good breakfast or supper.

MRS. RUNDELL
A New System of Domestic Cookery, 1806

PASTRY

Before the days of dietary domination by potatoes, pasta, and rice, it is not surprising that menus featured many hefty pies and tarts. Every cookbook offered a huge range of recipes for pastry or "paste" with varying quantities of flour, butter, sugar, cream, eggs, suet, and even ground rice or potatoes. Mrs. Austen gave Martha Lloyd two recipes for pastry made from butter and lard. These two, from Mrs. Rundell, are a little lighter.

———◦◉◦———

Shortcrust pastry

1¼ cups/170 g all-purpose (plain) flour

Pinch of salt

Scant stick/115 g unsalted butter (cold, from the fridge)

2–3 tbsp cold water

1 Put the flour and salt into a bowl.

2 Add the cold butter, then chop it with a knife until each piece of butter is as small as you can make it; along the way, make sure the butter pieces are thoroughly coated in flour. When you can chop no more, rub it in using just your fingertips; this keeps the mixture from becoming too warm, which may make it dense. Sprinkle in 2 tablespoons of cold water and mix it with a knife until it clumps together. Add a little more water if necessary. Bring it together with your hands to make a smooth dough, but don't knead it.

3 Cover it with plastic wrap (clingfilm) and let it rest in the fridge for 20 minutes before using.

4 When you are ready to use it, roll it out to an even thickness on a lightly floured surface.

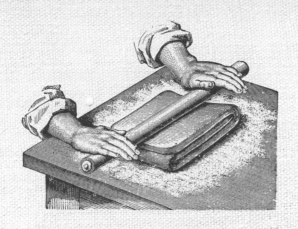

Sweet rich shortcrust pastry

1¾ cups/225 g all-purpose (plain) flour, plus extra for dusting

Pinch of salt

2 tsp superfine (caster) sugar

1 stick/125 g unsalted butter (cold, from the fridge)

1 egg yolk

3 tbsp cold water

1 Mix the flour, sugar, and salt in a bowl. Add the butter and chop and rub it in as in the previous recipe. Stir the cold water and egg yolk together, and add it to the flour and butter mixture. Use a knife to stir it so the mixture forms nice big clumps, adding a little more water if necessary. Bring it together with your hands to make a smooth dough, but don't knead it.

2 Wrap it in plastic wrap (clingfilm) and let it rest in the fridge for 20 minutes before using.

3 When you are ready to use it, roll it out on a lightly floured surface, handling it as little as possible to keep it cool.

Excellent Short Crust

Make two ounces of white sugar, pounded and sifted, quite dry; then mix it with a pound of flour well dried: rub into it three ounces of butter, so fine as not to be seen: into some cream put the yolks of two eggs, beaten, and mix the above into a smooth paste; roll it thin, and bake it in a moderate oven.

Another, Not Sweet But Rich

Rub six ounces of butter in eight ounces of fine flour; mix it into a stiffish paste, with as little water as possible; beat it well, and roll it thin. This, as well as the former, is proper for tarts of fresh or preserved fruits. Bake in a moderate oven.

INDEX

BIBLIOGRAPHY

Acton, Eliza, *Modern Cookery for Private Families*, London, 1845

Austen, Jane, *Emma*, ed Fiona Stafford, Penguin, London, 2003

    Lady Susan, The Watsons, Sanditon, ed Margaret Drabble, Penguin, London, 2003

    Mansfield Park, ed Kathryn Sutherland, Penguin, London, 2003

    Northanger Abbey, ed Marilyn Butler, Penguin, London, 2003

    Persuasion, ed Gillian Beer, Penguin, London, 2003

    Pride and Prejudice, ed Vivien Jones, Penguin, London, 2003

    Sense and Sensibility, ed Ros Ballaster, second edition, Penguin, London, 2003

    Minor Works, ed. R.W. Chapman, Oxford, revised edition, 1963

    Jane Austen's Letters, ed. R.W. Chapman, second edition, Oxford, 1979

Dods, Mistress Margaret (pseud. Christine Isobel Johnstone), *The Cook and Housewife's Manual: A Practical System of Modern Domestic Cookery and Family Management*, Edinburgh, 1826 (fifth edition, 1833)

Glasse, Hannah, *The Art of Cookery Made Plain and Easy* (by a Lady), London, 1747

Hickman, Peggy, *A Jane Austen Household Book*, with Martha Lloyd's recipes, David and Charles, London, 1977

Raffald, Elizabeth, *The Experienced English Housekeeper*, Manchester, 1769

Rundell, Maria Eliza, A New System of Domestic Cookery, John Murray, London, 1806 (revised edition 1816)

Verral (also spelled Verrall), William, A Complete System of Cookery, London, 1759

ACKNOWLEDGMENTS

Thanks to Jane Austen's House Museum and to David and Charles for their kind permission to reproduce the version of Martha Lloyd's recipes from *A Jane Austen Household Book*, which have been written out and rationalized by Peggy Hickman; and to Oxford University Press for their kind permission to quote from Jane Austen's letters from their edition by R.W. Chapman.

Renewed thanks to those excellent cooks who generously gave their advice, expertise, and time testing those recipes from *Dinner with Mr Darcy* that have been reproduced here: Mariateresa Boffo-O'Kane, Isabelle de Cat, Sarah Christie, Ruth Segal, Phoebe Taplin, Jill Vogler, Emma Whiting; and to Jon Vogler for his elegant editorial suggestions. Thanks, too, to the talented team at CICO Books and to Peta Nightingale at LAW.